LEILA FLETCHER
MUSIC LESSONS HAVE BEGUN

TO THE TEACHER

There are two practice habits which are of utmost importance to the beginner. They are the basis of piano technique and good musicianship. One is the habit of LISTENING when playing, and the other that of playing WITH EASE (without stiffness or tension.) BOTH MUST BE CULTIVATED FROM THE VERY FIRST LESSON. The beginner should play with a soft, musical tone. The hands should feel natural and comfortable on the keyboard.

The following presentation of lesson material is recommended because it is very simple, each new musical fact being taught separately, and because it is designed to CONCENTRATE THE ATTENTION ON TONE and EASE IN PLAYING.

1. Teach the finger-numbers: 1, 2, 3, 4, 5.

2. Have the pupil play different piano keys, (*any* keys of his own choosing) first with finger 3 of the right hand, then with left hand, finger 3; then right hand finger 2; then left hand finger 2, and so on, the teacher asking for the number-names of the fingers the pupil will use.

3. Teach by imitation a legato, three-note exercise, played by the strong fingers, 3, 2, and 1, on *any three* consecutive white keys. For example: Right hand, playing in the treble part of the keyboard, keys: A, G, F, G, A; (*or any three keys*) fingering: 3, 2, 1, 2, 3. Then left hand, playing in the bass part of the keyboard, keys: D, E, F, E, D; fingering: 3, 2, 1, 2, 3. Allow the pupil to play any three consecutive keys he happens to choose. (The pupil does not, as yet, know the letter-names of the piano keys.)

Now teach the same exercise using the reverse fingering, 1, 2, 3, 2, 1, each hand, and playing any three consecutive keys as before.

4. On the KEYBOARD teach D between the *two* black keys. Have the pupil find and play several different D's. Then teach C, D, E,—one key on each side of D, the "melody" *rising*. Drill: "Play C, D, E with right hand, fingers 1, 2, 3. Say the letter-names of the keys as you play. Find and play C, D, E in different places on the piano." "Play C, D, E with left hand, fingers 3, 2, 1, in different places on the piano." Then show Middle C (close to the lock on the piano) and ask the pupil to play Middle C, D, E.

5. Next, teach BY IMITATION the little piece entitled "C-D-E" on page 6. *Do not show the pupil the music.* Play "C-D-E" and sing the words; then have the pupil imitate, playing and singing the words. "C-D-E" is a piece for the RIGHT HAND ONLY. It is NOT to be played by the left hand. (*The reason for this is that we are soon going to teach "C-D-E" from the notes and we want the pupil to associate the printed notes of "C-D-E" with the right hand.*)

Copyright, MCMXLVII, by The Boston Music Co.

International Copyright Secured

6. On the KEYBOARD, as the pupil already knows **C**, it is easy to teach C, B, A, the "melody" *falling*. Drill on playing C, B, A, in different places on the keyboard, using the left hand fingers 1, 2, 3; right hand fingers 3, 2, 1.

7. Next teach BY IMITATION the piece entitled "C-B-A" on page 7. "C-B-A" is a LEFT HAND piece and is NOT to be played by the right hand.

   (*This is usually enough material for the first lesson for the average pupil of six or seven years of age—in which case the pupil should write the words of "C-D-E" and "C-B-A" in his writing book for use when playing at home. The melodies are more easily recalled than the words. If the teacher considers it necessary, the pupil may also write the letter-names of the notes, using a dash which may be called a "hold" for the two-beat notes, in this way: C, D, E—, C, D, E—, C, D, E, D, C, D, C—.*)

   (*Note: Very young pupils may be taught the first four bars only, of each piece, at the first lesson—"C-D-E has a tree."—and "C-B-A likes to play."*)

8. On the KEYBOARD teach A, B, C, D, E, F, G. (Review the keyboard for several lessons to make sure that the pupil has it clearly in mind, and can find any key without hesitation.)

9. Now show the diagram of the Grand Staff on page 4. Draw attention to the Treble Staff for notes from Middle C UP, which are played by the right hand, and to the Bass Staff for notes from Middle C DOWN, which are played by the left hand. Then on page 5, show and name—do not go into involved explanations—the one-count note, the two-count note, the bar lines dividing the music into bars, the Upper figure of the Time Signature which tells how many counts, or beats, there are in each bar, and the Lower figure of the Time Signature which shows that this note ♩ receives one count. (As simple time, in which the crotchet is the unit of measurement, is the only kind of time which should concern the beginner, (²⁄₄, ³⁄₄, ⁴⁄₄) the explanation of the *lower* figure of the time signature may be left until later in music study.)

10. The pupil is now ready to play "C-D-E" and "C-B-A" on pages 6 and 7 from the notes, 1st, playing and "saying" the notes; 2nd, playing and counting aloud; 3rd, playing and singing, or saying, the words; 4th, playing with the attention concentrated on the tone.

From now on, all pieces should be learned from the notes. (*For very young children, however, the rote-then-note procedure may be continued.*)

The first seven pieces (and two little exercises called "Music Games") employ only fingers 1, 2, and 3, so that the pupil will have practice in using the strong fingers before going on to pieces requiring the use of the weaker, more difficult, 4th and 5th fingers. In the pieces that follow, notes played by the 4th and 5th fingers are introduced gradually and in a way which makes their use as easy and natural as possible.

DUETS: A second-part has been provided for a number of pieces, to give training in ensemble playing—thereby developing a stronger feeling for rhythm, harmony, and interpretation. The piano solo part is, however, complete without this second part and these pieces may all be used either as solos or duets.

THE MELODY LINE: Single note pieces, with the melody divided between the hands, offer an excellent opportunity for developing the left hand *equally with the right hand* in melody playing and expression.

MEMORIZING MUSIC: Each lesson assignment should contain some memory work. The musical memory grows with cultivation. (Memorizing is one of the best forms of ear-training.)

LINES and SPACES: The lines and spaces in treble and bass should be memorized OUTWARDS from Middle C. Many teachers teach the bass notes outwards as far down on the staff as F or E and then revert to the obsolete and confusing method of memorizing the bass lines and spaces upwards! Bass lines and spaces must be memorized DOWNWARDS: A-F-D-B-G, and G-E-C-A. The pupil will then be able to read all notes on the staff simply by co-relating staff and keyboard; he will be able to "locate" notes on the keyboard without any doubt; and notes on leger lines below the bass staff will be easy to read and to place on the keyboard. (*The lowest line of the bass staff, G, is the fifth line, not the first line as it is often wrongly called; and the highest line, A, is the first line.*)

CONTENTS

NAMES OF KEYS ON THE PIANO KEYBOARD

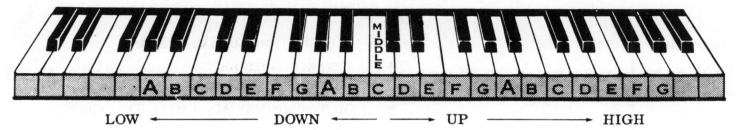

LOW ← → DOWN ← → UP → HIGH

TO THE PUPIL

GOOD PLAYING CONDITIONS

The chair should be the *right height,* so that the hand and fore-arm are *about level*.

The feet rest on the floor. If the feet do not reach the floor, use a foot-rest.

The fingers should be curved, but not too much. The thumb plays on its side, and should be over the keyboard. The wrist should be *loose*.

The music should be placed below eye-level, *not above*. If necessary, use a music rack or any device to lower the music.

Practise in a *good light*.

The piano should be kept well tuned.

PIANO KEYS

When piano keys are depressed, they drop less than $\frac{1}{2}$ inch! Therefore, it is EASY to play the piano.

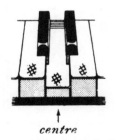

centre

Play in the *centre* of each key, not near the side.

GRAND STAFF

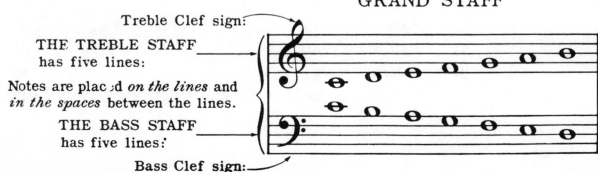

Treble Clef sign:

THE TREBLE STAFF has five lines:

Notes are placed *on the lines* and *in the spaces* between the lines.

THE BASS STAFF has five lines:

Bass Clef sign:

Notes from Middle C UP are written on the treble staff.

Notes from Middle C DOWN are written on the bass staff.

TIME VALUES OF NOTES

♩ receives 1 count
(crotchet, 1 beat)

♩ receives 2 counts
(minim, 2 beats)

♩· receives 3 counts
(dotted-minim, 3 beats)

○ receives 4 counts
(semibreve, 4 beats)

LETTER NAMES OF NOTES

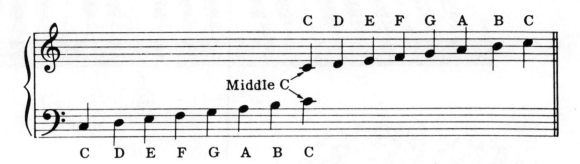

Middle C

C D E F G A B C

C D E F G A B C

This is how the fingers are numbered for playing the piano:

left hand

Thumbs are ONE!

right hand

THE TIME SIGNATURE: At the beginning of a piece of music you will see *two figures*, $\frac{2}{4}$,–or $\frac{3}{4}$,–or $\frac{4}{4}$, placed after the treble clef and also after the bass clef. These two figures are called the TIME SIGNATURE. The UPPER figure tells how many counts, or beats, there are *in each bar of the piece.* The lower figure tells that this note ♩ receives one count.

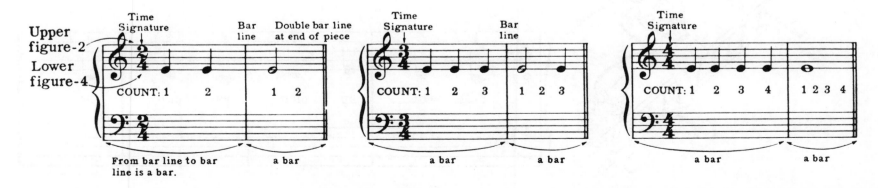

Right Hand notes

C D E

C-D-E

C - D - E has a tree,

Full of ap - ples as can be.

Left Hand notes

A B C

C-B-A

C - B - A likes to play,

In the mea - dow on the hay.

MUSIC GAME 1:
"Play and Say" 5 times
(Play, and say the letter-names.)

C D E D C E C;

C B A B C A C.

Right Hand notes

Left Hand notes

Marching

MARCHING – Second Part

(For Teacher, or slightly
advanced pupil.)

Right hand

Left hand

R.H.

L.H.

March - ing,　　march - ing,　　pom,　pom,　　pom!

Hear　us　　beat　the　　big　bass　　drum!

Gallop Away

New Time Signature: $\frac{3}{4}$
The three-count note: 𝅗𝅥.

Gal - lop a - way! Whis - tle a tune!

Off in the morn - ing and back by noon!

MUSIC GAME 2:
"Play and Say" 5 times

E D C   E   D   C

A B C   A   B   C

The Rainbow

THE RAINBOW—Second Part

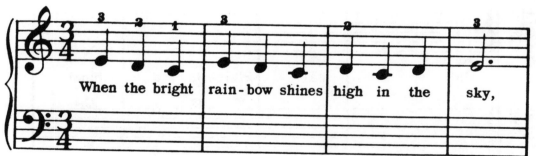

When the bright rain-bow shines high in the sky,

Rain-drops are smil-ing and say-ing good-bye!

BABY BEAR—Second Part

New Time Signature: 4/4
Four-count note: o

Baby Bear

Once there was a ba-by bear;

He lived in a hol-low tree; When the day was

bright and fair, His dain-ty nose you'd see.

Note: Later, "Baby Bear" may be played with fingers 2,3,4; and later again, with fingers 3,4,5.

Autumn Song

Au-tumn days are here a - gain, Down the leaves come fall - ing;

Leaves of red and leaves of gold, Heed the north wind's call - ing.

Right Hand notes

Left Hand notes

Hiking

MUSIC GAME 3:
"Play and Say" 5 times

My dog, Boots, and I go hik-ing on a sum-mer day;

Through the woods and down the hill, we wan-der far a - way.

C D E F   C E F

C B A G   C A G

C major scale.

R.H.	①	2	3	①	2	3	4	5	4	3	2	①	3	2	1
	C	D	E	F	G	A	B	C	B	A	G	F	E	D	C
L.H.	5	4	3	2	①	3	2	①	2	3	①	2	3	4	5

My Clock

The Chimes

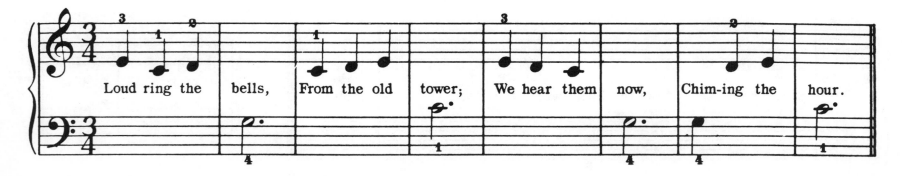

My Pony

French Folk Song

Trot a -long my po - ny, up the hills and down; Trot a -long my po - ny, can-ter in-to town.

MY PONY – Second Part

R. H.

L. H.

1.   2.

Good Pier-rot is wait - ing, at the vil - lage fair;

Trot a - long my po - ny, we will soon be there.

YANKEE DOODLE—Second Part

Yankee Doodle

Yan - kee Doo - dle came to town, A - rid - ing on a po - ny;

Stuck a feath - er in his cap, And called it Mac - a - ro - ni.

My Aeroplane

How I'd like to | go a - fly-ing, | high up in the | sky;

But my plane will | nev - er go, 'twill | nev - er real - ly | fly.

The Sail-Boat

Sail, lit - tle | boat, | o - ver the | sea; | Come, lit - tle | boat, | home-ward to | me.

THANKSGIVING HYMN—Second Part

THE PHRASE in music may be likened to *a line* in a verse of poetry. In music, the phrase is marked by a slur ⌒. For example, the phrases are marked in this "Thanksgiving Hymn." The words in the piano songs in this book show you the phrases. Each line of words in the verse is a phrase. Try to make your playing sing the words.

Thanksgiving Hymn

Folliott S. Pierpont
(Adapted)

Spanish Chant

For the beau-ty | of the earth, | For Thy gifts of | count-less worth; | For the day and | for the night,

Sun and moon and | stars of light, | Lord of all, to | Thee we raise, | This our song of | grate-ful praise.

Bugles

Bugles blow - ing o - ver the hill,

Hear the ech - oes ring - ing still!

MUSIC GAME 4:
"Play and Say" 5 times

Bugle Call

F A F A   C C C

C A C A   F F F

Good King Wenceslas

English Christmas Carol

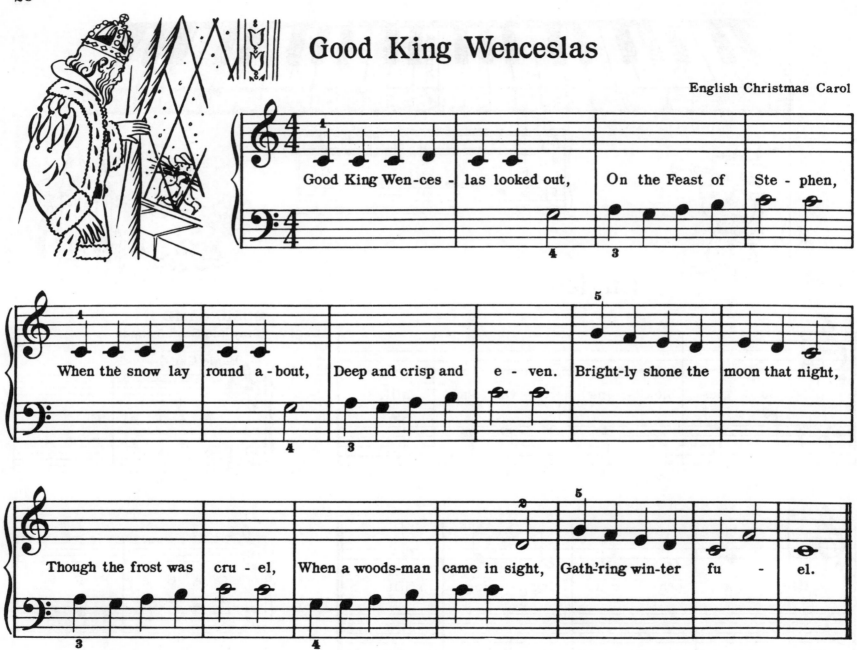

Train Whistle Exercise:
Play hands together!

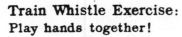

play softly

The four-count rest ▬

THE TRAIN–Second Part

The Train

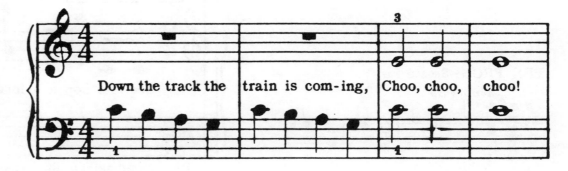

Down the track the | train is com-ing, | Choo, choo, | choo!

Wheels are hum-ming, | en-gine thrum-ming, | Toot-toot-toot, | toot!

The Frog

♫ = 1 count.
These notes are
two-to-a-count
notes.

Arr. from J. Haydn

THE FROG—Second Part

p *non legato*

See him hop a - long the log, Hap-py lit-tle ba-by frog!

Say: *Run*-ning, *run*-ning, *run*-ning, *walk!*

Soon he'll take a long-er jump, From the high-est, hick-'ry stump!

The Duckling

German Folk Song

MUSIC GAME 5:

Here is "Borrowed D"–the *left hand* plays D *above* Middle C.

"Play and Say" 5 times

G A B C D B D

"Borrowed"
D

Lit - tle down - y duck-ling, bet - ter hur - ry off to school,

Hur - ry off to school; You must learn to swim and dive, down in the shad - y

pool. You must learn to swim and dive, down in the shad - y pool.

EVENING HYMN - Second Part

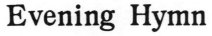

Evening Hymn

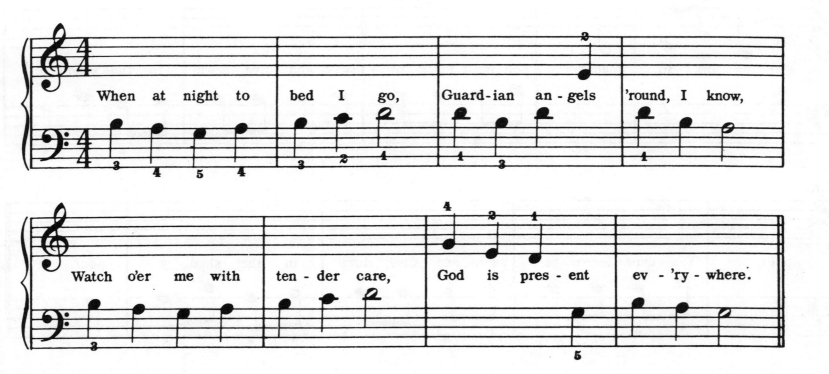

When at night to bed I go, Guard-ian an - gels 'round, I know,

Watch o'er me with ten - der care, God is pres - ent ev - 'ry - where.

WHAT SHALL I SING? – Second Part

F#

When the SHARP sign ♯ is placed before a note, play the black key *higher* on the piano, to the *right* of the white key, *in place of the white key*.

What Shall I Sing?

KEEP YOUR WRISTS UP !!

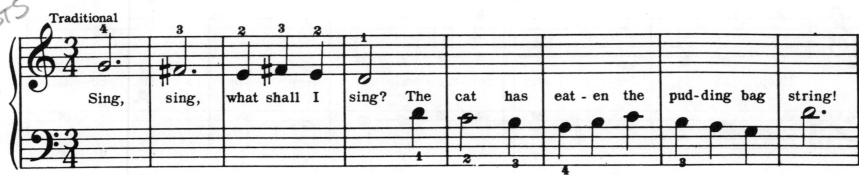

Traditional

Sing, sing, what shall I sing? The cat has eat-en the pud-ding bag string!

Do, do, what shall I do? The cat has eat-en it quite in two!

OLD MACDONALD HAD A FARM – Second Part (for page 27)

The two-count rest
The one-count rest

Sleep, Baby, Sleep

German Folk Song

Sleep, ba - by, sleep; Our cot - tage vale is deep; The lit - tle lamb is

on the green, With wool - ly fleece, so soft and clean; Sleep, ba - by, sleep.

The Sharp sign, used *once* in the bar, makes all notes of *the same letter-name* sharp:

Old MacDonald Had a Farm

Action Song

Old Mac-Don-ald had a farm, E - I - E - I - O! And on the farm he

had some chicks, E - I - E - I - O! A chick, chick here, a chick, chick there, And

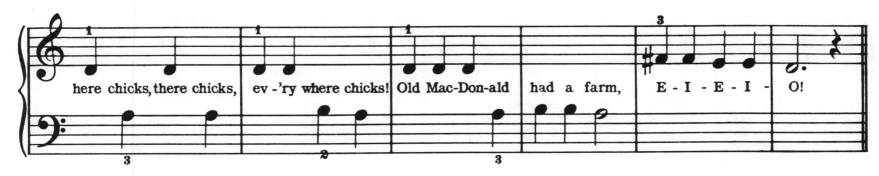

here chicks, there chicks, ev-'ry where chicks! Old Mac-Don-ald had a farm, E - I - E - I - O!

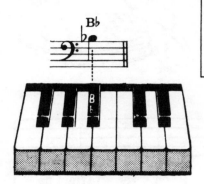

When the FLAT sign ♭ is placed before a note, play the black key *lower* on the piano, to the *left* of the white key, *in place of the white key*.

The Flat sign, used *once* in the bar, makes all notes of *the same letter-name* flat:

B♭ B♭

Twinkle, Twinkle

French

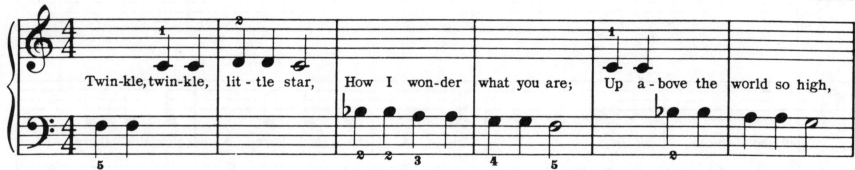

Twin-kle, twin-kle, lit - tle star, How I won-der what you are; Up a-bove the world so high,

Like a dia-mond in the sky. Twin-kle, twin-kle, lit - tle star, How I won-der what you are.

The Hallowe'en Pumpkin

French Folk Song
(Adapted)

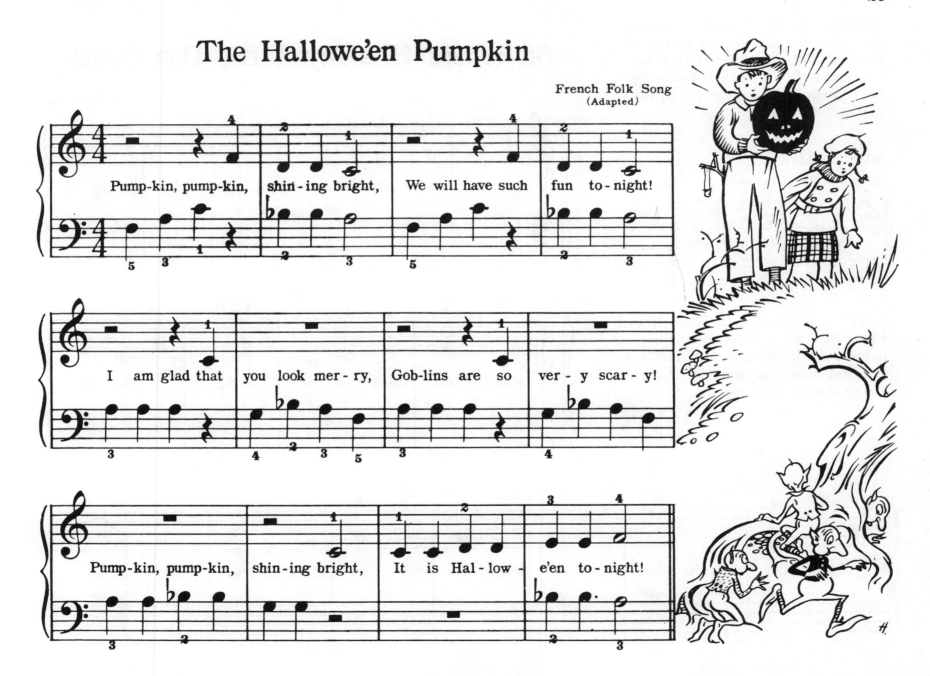

Pump-kin, pump-kin, shin-ing bright, We will have such fun to-night!

I am glad that you look mer-ry, Gob-lins are so ver-y scar-y!

Pump-kin, pump-kin, shin-ing bright, It is Hal-low-e'en to-night!

This piece begins with an *incomplete bar*. It begins on the *third beat* of the bar. The incomplete bar at the beginning of the piece is balanced by the incomplete bar at the *end* of the piece.

MUSIC GAME 6:

"Play and Say" 5 times

A TIE is a curved line between two consecutive notes of the *same letter-name*, in the same position on the staff. Play the first note *only*, and *hold it* for the time value of *both* notes:

Oh Where Has My Little Dog Gone?

Traditional

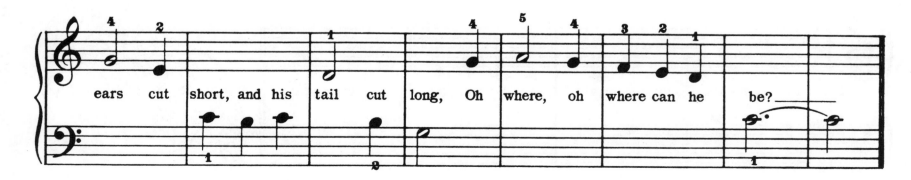

The Donkey

There's a don - key tied by the old oak tree, And he shakes his head and he laughs at me; I feed him ap - ples oats and hay, And he shakes his head, and he laughs all day! Hee - haw! Hee-haw! Hee - haw!

The PAUSE

When the pause is placed over or under a note ( ) hold the note *longer than its time value*. In "The Donkey," hold the notes marked by the pause long enough to make the braying of the donkey sound real.

Camp-Fire March

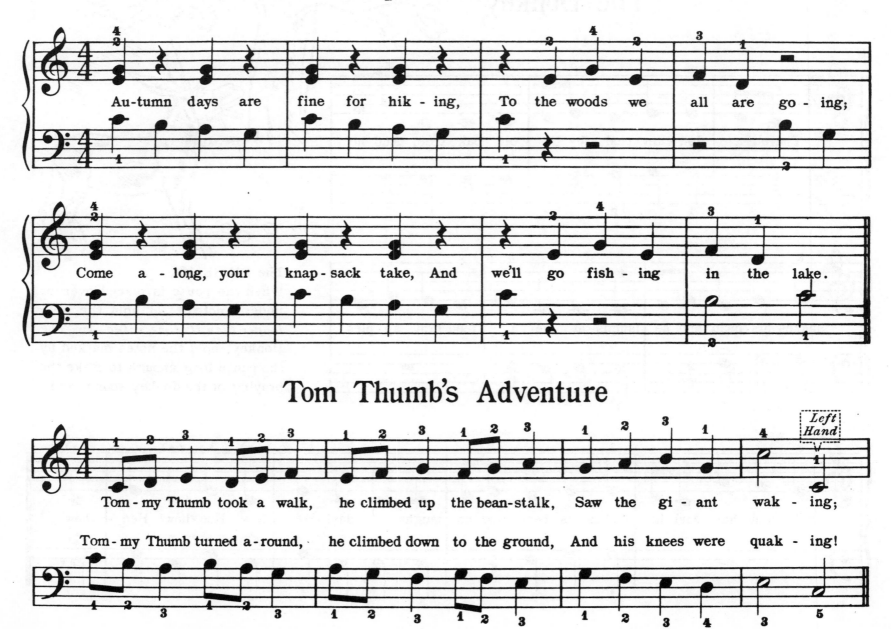

Tom Thumb's Adventure

Canoe Song

Float - ing in my birch can - oe,

This is what I love to do.

Pad - dle, pad - dle,

all a - long, Lis - ten to the riv - er's song.

My Bonnie

College Song

MUSIC GAME 7:

"Play and Say" 5 times

My Bon-nie sailed o-ver the o-cean,___ My Bon-nie sailed o-ver the sea;___ My Bon-nie sailed o-ver the o-cean,___ Oh bring back my Bon-nie to me.

E G B G E

MUSIC GAME 8:

Here is "Borrowed" E
the left hand plays E
above Middle C.

"Play and Say" 5 times

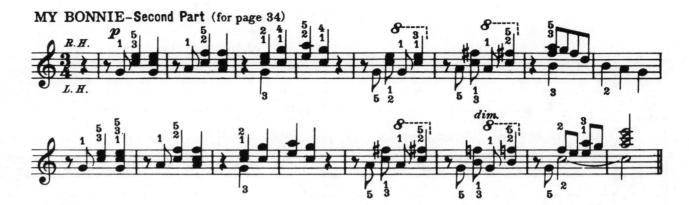

MY BONNIE—Second Part (for page 34)

The Blacksmith

Christmas Bells

Hear the bells of Christ-mas ring-ing, Joy-ful car-ols they are sing-ing, Hap-py bells of Christ-mas Day.

At Yuletide

The sharp, placed on the line F, *just after the treble clef and after the bass clef* is called the KEY SIGNATURE. The Key Signature shows that the note F is to be played *F sharp* throughout the piece.

Good King Wen-ces-las looked out, Sil-ver chimes were ring-ing;

AT YULETIDE
Second Part

And the song-sters round a-bout, Car-ols all were sing-ing.

MERRILY – Second Part

Merrily

Old Song

Mer - ri - ly we roll a - long, Roll a - long, roll a - long,

Mer - ri - ly we roll a - long, On the deep blue sea.

The Semibreve Rest is used for a *bar* of silence in any kind of time.

"Three Little Kittens" Exercise:

Play 5 times

PIERROT—Second Part (for page 39)

Three Little Kittens

Traditional

Three lit - tle kit-tens, they lost their mit-tens, And

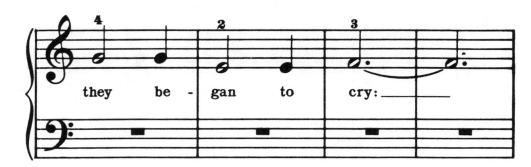

they be - gan to cry:

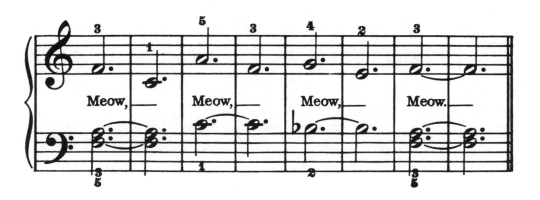

Meow, Meow, Meow, Meow.

Pierrot

French Folk Song

The flat, placed on the line B, *just after the treble clef and after the bass clef,* is called the KEY SIGNATURE. The Key Signature shows that the note B is to be played *B flat* throughout the piece.

The natural ♮.
The natural *cancels* the flat (or sharp). Play the *white key,* the natural key.

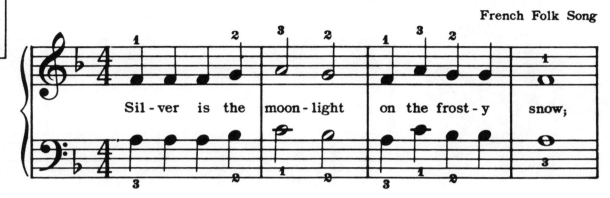

Sil - ver is the moon - light on the frost - y snow;

"At your door I'm knock - ing, my good friend, Pier - rot; I would write a let - ter,

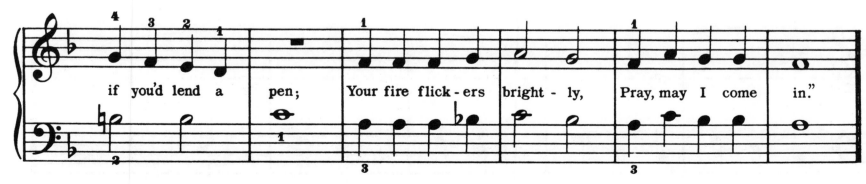

if you'd lend a pen; Your fire flick - ers bright - ly, Pray, may I come in."

The Rocking Horse

Follow the Leader

Come a - long, fol - low the lead - er, First take a look,

Then jump the brook! Fol - low up o - ver the hill - top,

O - ver the fence, and home!

Around the Totem Pole

(Tom-Tom)

At the Skating Rink

Skat - ers fly past us like this - tle - down fluff,

Um - pah, pah! um - pah, pah! Hear the town band! Cor - nets and trom - bones go

puff - et - ty - puff! Um - pah, pah! um - pah, pah! Skat - ing is grand!

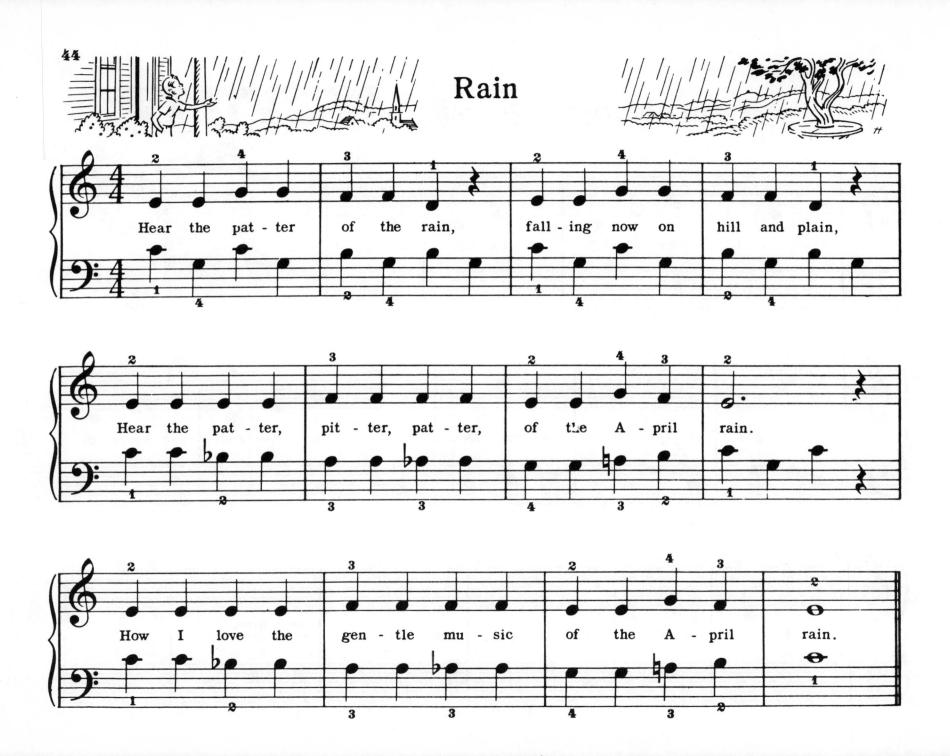

Rain

RED RIVER VALLEY – Second Part

Red River Valley

Key Signature,
two sharps–F♯,C♯.

Cowboy Song

Go a - long, go a - long, lit - tle po - ny,_____ O'er the moun - tains we on - ward must

roam; In the val - ley the camp-fire is glow-ing,_____ And a wel - come a - waits us at home.

THE ARKANSAS TRAVELLER – Secondo

Morning Song

German Folk Song

Song of a lark in the dawn - ing, Gold - en the rays of the sun,

Flow - ers with dew-drops are nod - ding, Sweet - ly the day is be - gun.

The ACCENT sign >
Play the *accented* note
a little *louder*

Stems UP– play with right hand
Stems DOWN– play with left hand

The Arkansas Traveller

American Traditional

Primo
Fairly fast